God's Call
to
Public Responsibility

EDITORS

George W. Forell

William H. Lazareth

JUSTICE

BOOKS

FORTRESS PRESS   PHILADELPHIA

Library of Congress Cataloging in Publication Data

Main entry under title:
God's call to public responsibility.

   (Justice books)
   Bibliography: p.
   1. Christianity and justice—Addresses, essays,
lectures, I. Forell, George Wolfgang. II. Lazareth,
William Henry, 1928-   III. Series.
BR115.J8G63   261.8'3   77-78651
ISBN 0-8006-1551-4

6458I77   Printed in the United States of America   1-1551

Contents

Regular contributors to Justice Books, in addition to the editors, include Charles V. Bergstrom, Elizabeth A. Bettenhausen, George H. Brand, John A. Evenson, Franklin D. Fry, Franklin L. Jensen, Foster R. McCurley, Richard J. Niebanck, Palmera B. Peralta, John H. Reumann, Lois M. Stormfeltz, Cedric W. Tilberg, Francis K. Wagschal, and Ruth C. Wick.

Government Limits to the "Free Exercise" of Religion

Paul G. Kauper

THE First Amendment of the United States Constitution provides that Congress "shall make no law respecting an establishment of religion or prohibiting the free exercise thereof." The Supreme Court has held that these limitations are applicable to the states also *via* the Fourteenth Amendment. Many state constitutions contain provisions directed toward the same ends, although not exactly the same results would be reached under them. We therefore have a rather widespread constitutional tradition in this country that emphasizes aspects of both religious liberty and limitations on state support of religion.

The establishment clause holds that the state should not support religion, or to put it positively, that religion must depend upon voluntary adherence and support. It is sometimes said that this establishment clause—in conjunction with the free exercise clause, or even without it—embodies implicitly the general principle of the separation of church and state. This is a broader principle than simply that the state shall *not* support religion, although the ideas overlap in large measure.

The other clause of the First Amendment says that Congress shall not pass any law prohibiting the free exercise of religion. This is more easily understood as placing restraints on the state against laws that burden or obstruct religious belief, worship, association, and conduct.

The late Paul G. Kauper was Professor of Constitutional Law at the Law School of the University of Michigan and author of such notable texts as *Cases and Materials on Constitutional Law*.

5

PRIMACY OF RELIGIOUS LIBERTY

According to one school of thought, both these clauses at the beginning of the First Amendment are really directed towards religious liberty. This is clearly manifest in the free exercise clause, but on the surface it is not so clear in the establishment clause. By restraining the power of government to support or intervene in religious matters however, the establishment clause serves to reinforce and strengthen the free exercise limitation.

Moreover, when the establishment clause is viewed in this perspective it affords some interesting insights into problems of its interpretation. It should not be given a construction that denigrates or belittles religious liberty, but rather one that harmonizes with religious liberty or is even subordinated to this end. In other words, the separation principle is not an ultimate one in American constitutional life, but an instrumental idea designed to serve the broad interest of religious liberty.

TESTS FOR STATE AID

The Supreme Court has dealt with a series of cases involving governmental financial assistance for church-related institutions. While interpreting the intent and limits of the establishment clause, the Court has developed a number of ideas it has at varying times used as tests or guidelines—without any great degree of consistency.

(1) *"Wall of Separation."* In an early opinion the Court said the establishment clause sets up an alleged "wall of separation" (Jefferson) between church and state. This precludes not just an established church preferentially receiving government aid; it also prohibits all aid to religion and proscribes any use of tax monies to support religious education.

It was obvious at the time—and became increasingly apparent—that understanding the establishment clause as forbidding all aid to religion was much too broad an interpretation. Taken at its face value, it is simply an untenable proposition. The free exercise clause of the First Amendment has not been excised by the establishment clause. Among other things, it assures that the Government will protect the free exercise of religion and assures the conditions that make it possible. This is probably the most significant aid the state gives to religion. All broad propositions relating to the establishment clause must constantly be balanced off against the requirements of the free exercise clause.

Indeed, to further the idea of religious liberty, the Court has also said that the state may accommodate its policies to the religious interests of the people. It may take them distinctively into account in its programs so as not to interfere with the freedom of people to pursue their religious interests. This line of cases goes so far as to suggest that the state may deliberately cultivate a program that makes it more readily possible for people to pursue religious interests, even though this is not required in the name of the free exercise clause. I mention this simply to indicate that the no-aid proposition does not stand up.

Moreover—and perhaps this is the most important limitation— the Court has repeatedly said that the Government, in pursuing a secular program, may do so even though it has the incidental effect of aiding religion. Indirect aid is not forbidden. Thus, to cite a few cases, the Government may subsidize the transportation of children to church-related schools as well as to public schools, provide free textbooks of a secular character for children in parochial schools, enact a Sunday closing law that prohibits any work on Sunday, and provide assistance to help achieve the secular purposes of the church-related college. In all these cases it was evident that there were substantial incidental benefits that flowed into religious institutions or to the practice of religion, although these benefits were not sufficient to violate the establishment clause.

Perhaps even more striking is the granting of tax exemptions to churches with respect to property used for religious purposes. To some it may appear that the distinction between outright grants to churches on one hand and tax exemption on the other, is not clear. The Court, however, with only one judge dissenting, had no doubt that property used for religious purposes could be exempted from property taxes. This is indeed a very striking instance of the state's providing a form of economic aid—not merely to church-related enterprises, but to churches themselves. There was in this opinion a strong suggestion that perhaps such assistance was even required in the name of religious liberty—or at least that the Government, in order to avoid entanglements in church affairs that might imperil religious liberty, could appropriately decide to grant tax exemptions. Surely the decision represents an application of the so-called accommodation principle and again refutes the broad no-aid proposition.

Churches enjoy some of the most important privileges extended by the state, such as the right to incorporate. Thereby they gain the benefits of using the corporate entity for various purposes, including the ability to acquire and hold property in perpetuity. They also enjoy the benefit of the rules relating to charitable trusts, whereby unrestricted gifts may be made to churches and, again, held indefinitely. So in numerous ways the state, by extending to churches the benefit of its general laws—or at least the laws relating to nonprofit corporations—offers very distinctive "aid" to them.

(2) *Neutrality.*   Another idea that has been emphasized in these cases is "neutrality." The state must be neutral in dealing with religion. As Mr. Justice Harlan once observed, this is a very difficult concept to apply because there is no general understanding of the meaning of neutrality.

One very meaningful concept of neutrality that could have important implications for church-state relations is the idea that the state must deal with religion and religious institutions in an evenhanded way. This means that it may neither distinctively favor religious bodies nor discriminate against them. There is much to commend this evenhanded neutrality approach because of the simplicity underlying the concept and the relative simplicity of its application. According to this test, the Government may not enact laws or adopt programs that are determined by the religious factor or that either aid or inhibit religion.

Consider the case of aid to church-related institutions where the Government is pursuing a policy of aiding secular purposes. An evenhanded neutrality would require that the state not deny aid to church-related institutions that fit naturally into the general class benefited by the assistance. Thus, if educational benefits are extended to all educational institutions generally, it would be unconstitutional to deny them to church-related institutions on the theory that such aid would violate the establishment clause. Here an evenhanded policy would prohibit discrimination. It would not only authorize the legislature to deal evenhandedly but would also require it to do so—if this is the correct interpretation of these clauses. In other words: if churches could claim the benefits of the general class included, and if the class were nonprofit institutions generally, the church would also qualify.

If evenhandedness and lack of discrimination on the basis of religion are the criteria, there could be considerable relaxation of rules currently followed. For example, the Supreme Court sometimes requires states to discriminate on religious grounds in order to assure enjoyment of the free exercise benefits. Even though the establishment clause by itself may in some instances prohibit aid, regard for free exercise justifies the Government in pursuing these neutralizing aids. Here again it is the concept of "evenhandedness" that is aimed at reconciling the free exercise with the establishment clause. In practice, the superiority of free exercise over the establishment clause is actually asserted.

There is, however, another concept of neutrality that seems to have gained ascendancy in the Supreme Court. Often when justices speak of neutrality, they are not talking about evenhandedness or freedom from discrimination against religion in the dispensation of public benefits. The term *neutrality* is used by some justices as simply a restatement of the idea that the state must keep its hands off religion. In other words, instead of meaning evenhandedness, *neutrality* is interpreted to mean "that the state must keep its hands off religion and that it can do nothing either to benefit or to burden religion."

So stated, this becomes simply a reiteration of the idea that the Government cannot interfere with free exercise or do anything to aid religion. It is a dubious use of the concept of neutrality and one that adds nothing by way of new understanding. Thus when the Court in recent cases has declared that the establishment clause requires states to discriminate against parochial schools in the dispensation of benefits, it has assumed that this is consistent with its notion of neutrality. This rather curious notion of neutrality can hardly be squared with evenhandedness.

(3) *Triple Test.* The standard most frequently employed by the present Court is revealed in recent cases involving governmental programs that give assistance to teachers or parents of children attending parochial schools. In these cases the Court has developed a three-pronged test: (a) Is the legislation or program directed toward a secular purpose? (b) Does it have a primary effect that either advances or inhibits religion? (c) Does it create the risk of "excessive entanglements" between church and state?

The first prong of this test is the "secular purpose" of the state aid. Government may not concern itself with religious matters; it may not adopt programs to advance religion. It may not spend money distinctively aimed at religious purposes. It operates in a secular sphere and its objectives must all be stated in secular terms.

It is noteworthy that the Court in recent cases has declared with no difficulty that providing the elements of a general education to children in parochial schools or in colleges easily fits the secular-purpose idea. It does not challenge the view that a legislature may be spending money for secular ends even when it extends the benefits of its spending policies to include church-related institutions. The real difficulty comes with the remaining two parts of the test.

The second prong is the "primary effect" factor. Does aid have a primary effect that either advances or inhibits religion? It is on this ground that the Court in its more recent cases has invalidated programs of assistance to parochial schools which aid the parents and children who attend them. Thus the Court has held invalid such practices as direct grants to schools for maintenance and repair of their facilities, direct grants to schools designated to reimburse them for giving tests mandated by state law, tuition grants to parents sending their children to parochial schools, and tax deductions to parents for tuition costs incurred in sending their children to parochial schools.

These cases have almost completely demolished the possibility of any assistance to either parochial schools or to the parents of children attending them—although bus transportation and text-books apparently are still available as permissible forms of aid.

We are interested in the Court's analysis in terms of the tests stated. It acknowledged that there was a secular purpose, and it did not doubt that this was achieved by the programs. On the other hand, since these schools were sectarian in character, one of their principal purposes was to insure sectarian instruction, and since all their programs were infused with religious features, the state could not achieve its secular purpose without at the same time advancing a religious objective. Aid therefore had the primary effect of advancing religion even though the forms of aid—assistance to parents through tuition reimbursement and tax deduction devices—were indirect. The Court said that even in these cases there was an encouragement to parents to send their children to schools which had a predominantly sectarian character. Consequently, the program had "a direct and primary effect" of aiding religion and was therefore unconstitutional.

At the same time, the Court in several cases has held that because church colleges are not so completely infused with sectarian objectives and can be seen to serve primarily secular purposes, capital grants to them which assist in putting up buildings to be used for secular teaching do not violate the establishment clause.

Thus the Court gets itself involved in the complexities of distinguishing between the primary objects of a program by determining whether the secular purpose will be served without substantially aiding religious purposes. In some respects, the net result of this primary effect test is a return to the old idea that the state can do nothing to aid religion. Nevertheless, the Court continues to recognize that an aid which is simply incidental to a secular purpose is constitutional.

It is obvious that there is a good deal of rhetoric here. The tests used by the Court are not sufficiently stringent. When is aid incidental to a secular purpose, and when is it direct and primary aid to religion even though at the same time it furthers a substantially secular purpose?

The third prong of the test is "excessive entanglements," a fac-

tor the Court has added only in recent years. Its general idea is
that church and state should be kept separate and the civil
Government should not interfere with religious authorities in administering religious institutions.

The Court first applied this idea in the tax exemption case. It
said the state might well decide to grant exemptions to church
bodies in order to avoid the excessive entanglements that might
arise if the attempt were made to tax churches. If all the usual in-
cidents of the taxing power were exercised, it would result in a
considerable intrusion by Government into the affairs of
churches.

This idea was applied then by the Court in parochial aid cases.
The Court held that paying teachers to teach secular subjects
fulfilled a proper secular purpose. Nevertheless, because of the in-
fusion of religion into the whole program, it would be necessary
for the state to engage in constant surveillance of the teaching
financed by these public funds in order to be sure such funds were
not directed toward sectarian purposes.

Thus excessive entanglements have entered the picture; they
are a significant factor and a valid consideration. Although there
is some overlapping of functions between church and state, it is
desirable in the interest of protecting the integrity of both that
one not interfere in the affairs of the other.

The difficulty lies in applying this concept, since obviously
there are many entanglements between church and state. Programs and operations of the churches entail secular aspects such
as the acquisition and control of property through the maintenance of church facilities. In such cases the state is already entangled in the affairs of the church. A church can be sued for
breach of contract. A church is subject to zoning restrictions and
building restrictions of various kinds, and its failure to comply
may result in legal entanglements. Even in the sphere of educational affairs, the state has already entangled itself in church-
related institutions in a substantial way by various educational
requirements it prescribes for schools and colleges.

It is not a question, therefore, whether there are entanglements. The question is whether these entanglements require civil
authorities to make determinations that intrude on religious

autonomy. Perhaps the issue can best be approached in terms of whether and to what extent control is needed in proportion to the aid that is given.

It is easily possible to exaggerate the surveillance required to police governmental subsidies in order to assure achievement of the secular purpose. It may seem somewhat fanciful to suggest that a civil officer must be present in a Roman Catholic classroom to see that the teacher of a secular subject does not intrude with religious considerations. No one suggests that it is necessary to have public authorities in a public school to see whether a teacher is using the classroom to advance secularism or any other kind of ideology equally offensive under the establishment clause.

I am not suggesting that this should be the case. I am simply indicating that the Court seems to apply special criteria in dealing with the problem of excessive entanglements where the parochial schools are involved. On the other hand, the Court has said that so far as church-related colleges are concerned, unless it is shown that they are closed schools in a strict sectarian sense, excessive surveillance will not be required to insure that grants made for secular purposes are limited to secular use.

The upshot of this theory is that it is permissible for the Government to grant assistance to church-related hospitals, since they are seen to serve primarily secular purposes and any aid to religion is incidental in character. Aid to a church-related college is also valid, provided that the institution is not infused with such a high degree of sectarianism that extensive surveillance is required in order to assure achievement of the secular purpose. On the other hand, the Court has almost completely demolished any possibility of giving direct or even indirect assistance to parochial schools by allowing tax benefits to parents or providing for tuition reimbursements. The Court finds that even this indirect assistance is a direct and primary aid to religion because of the sectarian aspects of these schools.

It is obvious from these decisions that the Court makes no pretense of neutrality in any evenhanded sense. Indeed, it has explicitly said that the requirements of free exercise and freedom from discrimination are subordinate to the requirements of the establishment clause. One of the difficult questions this raises is:

When does the Court find that establishment is subordinate to free exercise and vice versa? What historical, philosophical, or constitutional considerations have led the Court to conclude that the establishment limitation is more important than the free exercise limitation?

This is not the occasion to examine those questions, except to suggest that the Court's conclusions are not required either by history, by precedent, or by any compelling language of establishment. Instead, they represent basic policy predilections. It is particularly regrettable that the Court has not seen fit to give serious thought to neutrality in any meaningful sense of the word. The Court has not carefully weighed the competing demands of religious liberty in finding that the establishment clause prohibits aid to these institutions for secular purposes.

The Court had a great opportunity in the "excessive entanglements" cases to draw a line between assistance that is direct and primary to sectarian institutions and that which is indirect and offers no threat to excessive entanglements. It missed a great opportunity to bring constitutional interpretation in line with the contemporary situation and the pluralistic character of our society.

These constitutional and other legal problems raised by governmental assistance to church-related institutions cannot be concluded without reference to another problem which hovers in the picture. That is the place of religion in the public order.

PRIVATIZATION OF RELIGION

The church recognizes that both the state and the church are part of God's rule and that the church is distinctively here to serve a religious function. The church declares God's law for all men as part of the created order and recognizes the state as an instrument for social justice. The church also bears witness to the gospel of Christ's work for human redemption.

It is useful to emphasize that the church really has a dual function in its spiritual capacity. Along with its priestly function, it also has a prophetic function to speak to the human condition which places humans as responsible creatures in the secular order. It is vitally concerned with God's requirement that justice be done among all persons. This is the basis of the church's interest in social issues and is appropriate to its preaching and teaching programs.

The church acknowledges the state's legitimacy and views it as an instrument in God's hands for achieving civil order, justice, and freedom. The church respects the state, prays for its leaders, and encourages its citizens to obey just laws. It also recognizes that the state is important for the church's ability to perform its own functions, in terms of preserving order, insuring religious liberty, and making it possible for the church to achieve its objectives within the regular legal order.

There is, therefore, no inherent conflict between church and state. Yet while recognizing the state and its legitimate authority, the church reserves judgment on whether the state has abused its power—and it may indeed stand in opposition to an unjust state, just as the Christian may in conscience refuse to obey laws he or she finds in conflict with faith.

How does the church make itself effective with respect to affairs of state in which it has a genuine, legitimate interest because of its concern with justice and freedom? Is the separation principle relevant here? Is the church required to abstain from passing judgment on matters of conscience in the public order? Are Christian citizens required to maintain a strict division between their religious faith on the one hand and public affairs on the other?

(1) *Religion a "Private Affair."*   In the course of an opinion dealing with parochial aid questions, Chief Justice Warren E. Burger expressed the common thought that religion is a "private affair," a matter for family, home, and church that should not intrude into the public domain. He made this remark in connection with the Court's assertion that the purpose of the constitutional principle is to keep religion from intruding into public debate and thereby creating divisiveness along religious lines.

Certainly the Chief Justice was totally wrong in his understanding, if he meant to say that religious considerations could never be adduced by churches and Christians in dealing with public affairs. Actually he was making a fairly narrow point. He was contending that it is well to withdraw some questions from the realm of public debate—although it may be doubted that it is the Court's function to serve as a censor to determine what may appropriately be considered in the public sector. Our more immediate concern, however, is to challenge the statement that religion is a private affair, a matter to be confined to the family and church.

If religion is essentially a private affair, then of course it can have nothing to say to matters in the public sector. According to this view, religion is concerned only with the salvation of souls, with the afterlife, and it cannot speak to the important issues of the present life. To suggest that this limitation on religion arises from the establishment clause is totally indefensible in view of the competing demand of the free exercise clause. In terms of that clause Christians are free to make witness, to win converts to the faith, and to express their positions on public policy from the Christian point of view—and the churches are also free both to exercise their prophetic function in matters of common concern and to bear witness to the gospel.

(2) *The Public Impact of Christians.*   First let us take the question of the viewpoint of the individual citizen and the impact of his religion on matters of public life. According to evangelical tradition, the most important way religion affects the public order is through the lives of dedicated Christians. While defending the right of religious freedom for all citizens, Christians will bring the qualities derived from their own faith into their daily life, into their thinking on matters of public order, and into the common melting pot of ideas that determine the public consensus and underlying moral conceptions informing the society. Hence Luther said that every Christian is to be a "little Christ to his neighbor."

Even short of that, however, a Christian is a responsible creature of God who feels an obligation to work for social justice, to serve his or her neighbors, to respect their rights, to obey the law, and to perform the duties of citizenship. Indeed, widespread acceptance of these conceptions of the constitutional order alone makes democracy possible.

It is wholly untenable to suggest that a person may not let religious faith illumine his or her conception of duty toward the neighbor, of the purposes the law ought to serve, of public policy objectives, or of proper respect for public office.

This would mean that one could split life into unrelated parts as a citizen and as a Christian. The notion of religion as a "private affair" (Burger) breaks down as soon as the state protects the free exercise of the kind of prophetic Christianity that calls for public involvement as part of the church's mission. Christ said his followers were to be the salt that seasons, the yeast that leavens, and the light that illumines. This indirect effect of Christian citizenship in relation to others is perhaps the most important of all elements in public life—surely in a democratic society. Here is the real impact of religion on matters of public interest.

To be sure: if Christianity is sterile, if it is strictly self-centered and self-seeking and lacks any sense of mission, it may not affect public life and will be totally irrelevant to the whole public order. However, to say that all "religion is strictly private" is to ignore a vital element of Christianity and to indicate a lack of perception in regard to the relation of religion to the public order.

(3) *The Church's Educational and Prophetic Role.* In cultivating the individual's faith, the church plays a vital part in influencing the public order. To the extent that it succeeds in cultivating a faith that has a genuine ethical concern about man's dealings with his neighbors—a faith that is concerned with justice, freedom, and the general public interest, and that creates in its membership a readiness to assume civic obligations—the church is making an impact on the public order which can not be lightly discounted.

For this reason the church is properly interested in the study of the Bible with respect to its conception of justice and of the duties owed to one's neighbors. It is also concerned with encouraging the study of contemporary problems from the viewpoint of Christian ethics and encouraging citizens to take an interest in these matters. Likewise, the church can well say to its members that they may appropriately identify themselves with various civic groups that aim at secular political goals. There is no distinctively "Christian" answer to many questions that face us, and there are no detailed blueprints furnished by the Bible. There does arise from a Christian's faith in God, however, both a general appreciation of the righteous values served by the public order and a general sense of obligaton toward one's neighbors in society.

Perhaps a Christian's greatest obligation is to acquit himself or herself as a responsible citizen by examining questions, by bringing the best judgment to bear, and by drawing upon resources available to the community in respect to questions of policy that admittedly invite no single clear-cut answer, but conscientious thought and consideration. This is the best the Christian can do and it is his or her obligation.

What can the church do beyond educating its members and providing a medium for instruction in public issues to which the members' attention should be directed? Obviously the church also has a prophetic role to play with respect to social justice. And since it cannot be excluded from the public domain, religion is not a private matter. Through its organized facilities the church may devote time, effort, and money to undertake research on matters of public policy in order to help educate both its own members and the public at large. Its ministers may speak from the pulpit against sin wherever it raises its head, in public or private life, as part of the prophetic role of the church.

In addition, the church may in its corporate capacity adopt positions and resolutions dealing with matters that are in the public order. The freedom of the church to do this must be recognized as part of the free exercise of religion, and nothing in the establishment clause stands in its way. In doing so, however, the church must also exercise caution.

To the extent that it enters into the political arena and speaks on matters of political concern, some caveats must necessarily be observed. First, the church must speak out of sufficient knowledge in discussing matters of public concern.

Second, it must not purport to speak for all its members or to represent their points of view, when in fact there is room for division of opinion within its constituency on such matters. Church leaders may appropriately express their own views, and publicly represent the views officially adopted by their churches.

Third, the church must be careful not to impose upon others in our pluralistic society any sectarian views that conflict with the rights of others.

This introduces us to one of the most difficult questions of our day. In a pluralistic society like ours, how may any one group speak on religious matters in an effort to influence public policy? The state cannot use its legal institutions to force compliance with a religious view, or to force a religious view on people, or to give sanction in its laws to a religious dogma. This is part of our pluralistic freedom.

But pluralism suggests that various groups have something to contribute to the determination of public interest. Each group should be free to speak its mind. However, there is also the limitation that no group should attempt to impose its views on others at the expense of basic freedoms, or to secure laws that aim at essentially private matters and serve no important public interest.

Finally, the church should always rely on its processes of persuasion, rather than on such force and sanctions as it has through coercion of its members, to achieve its purposes. It is permissible for any group, including a church group, to proclaim its views on important questions that have great moral and ethical implications. Through the process of persuasion, in the arena of public debate, the church should seek to convince others to take its considerations into account in determining the fundamental concepts of a just public order.

Righteousness/Justice in Matthew (Series A)

Foster R. McCurley and John H. Reumann

To relate Scripture to justice for the church's ministry in today's world is no easy task. The intricacies of modern scholarship seem to many to get in the way of prophetic passion. Bible study, even though on the rise, is often inner-directed, toward individual growth or the dynamics of an already half-converted group, rather than directed to the world. The structures of the church seem also to be barriers, rather than conductors, in the efforts of the people of God to seek for justice and exercise their responsibility as brothers and sisters in Christ for sisters and brothers in creation.

Yet there are opportunities to relate Scripture with the social scene, to bind the divine economy with human economies, to connect the biblical books with bulging libraries of contemporary monographs and articles on psychology, ecology, and ethics, and to bring grace to bear on global as well as personal dilemmas. Indeed, it is often the gift of insights from historical scholarship which provides openings to see how the biblical witnesses speak concerning our problems today. Similarly, it is the liturgical opportunity at worship and the church's teaching ministry which give us a chance to explore biblical contributions to the task of achieving greater justices in life.

Biblically and homiletically, as well as in other ways, it will be the regular aim of these pages to suggest how *the Bible, as interpreted according to the best canons of hermeneutics in the church, can undergird, inspire, and lead our common work in quests for justice.*

Naturally these suggestions will have in mind such avenues open to every congregation of Christians as public worship, where the readings chosen from Scripture and elsewhere, the prayers, and the preaching are basic; proclamation generally, in the parish and beyond (to speak for justice at an ecumenical gathering, like the Week of Prayer for Christian Unity, or at a community occasion in our pluralistic society, is a chance to speak appropriately); and in the teaching and pastoral ministry, above all in Bible study groups.

We shall on occasion explore topics in contemporary social ethics from a biblical base. We shall at times examine how a text from the Bible has functioned in the understanding and pursuit of justice over the centuries. But especially we shall seek to link texts, on which preachers have preached and on which they are likely to preach currently, with today's wrenching agonies of injustice.

USING THE LECTIONARY

Of the many possible ways in which Scripture might be explored for our concerns with justice, in this first issue we shall concentrate on possibilities for preaching based on the lectionary assigned in most Lutheran, Roman Catholic, United States Episcopalian, and other churches in the first quarter of 1978. For public reading of the Bible and preaching on it are two of the most obvious ways in which the church reaches its people persuasively regarding justice.

The Three-Year Lectionary, based on the Roman *Ordo,* has the obvious advantage over previous lectionaries of putting more of the Bible into use triennially, compared with a system that used one set of lessons annually. Yet these lessons in the *Ordo,* it must be admitted, are not particularly well designed to further the interests of social ministry, ethics, or justice. That is so because the basic rationale is provided for many Sundays by the church year calendar, and on others by in-sequence reading of the Gospel for that year—for the ecclesiastical year beginning with Advent, 1977, St. Matthew.

All lectionaries have an internal structuring. The three-year set of lessons is built upon the principle that the Gospel for the Day is controlling. The Old Testament Lesson is chosen to support and amplify that Gospel passage. (In some cases the Old Testament verses are presented as a contrast to the Gospel passage. Only in rare cases does the Old Testament selection seem to stand in its own right.) The Epistle selection often reflects an in-sequence reading of a New Testament letter, as during Epiphany 2–8 in Year A, when 1 Corinthians 1–4 is read. When the church sets the tone, as in Lent, and the Gospels vary, the Epistles are more apt to have a connection with the other lessons, particularly the Gospel for the Day. But the rest of the year, the Epistle goes its own way, not directly related to Gospel or Old Testament choice. (For details see Contemporary Worship 6, *The Church Year: Calendar and Lessons [1973],* pp. 12–24.)

What does this structure of the lectionary have to do with concern for justice? If it be granted that the Old Testament is more likely to be concerned with justice than the New—in part because the eschatological situation in the New does not often look to developing social-ethical involvements, and in part because the Old, with its greater bulk and longer centuries of involvement in the world, developed far more in the way of legislation for justice and prophetic outcry for rights—then the Old Testament, if it is always read in subservience to the Gospel for the Day, is not likely to be reflected in the lectionary to the degree that it contains "justice passages." But this general observation needs to be tested by examining actual cases *with an eye to seeing how the lectionary choices can be said to speak on social concerns.*

To symbolize the orientation of the lectionary to the Gospel for the Day at the expense of the Old Testament, we shall here treat the New Testament first and then the Old.

A corollary to all this is that the Epistles, insofar as they are apropos to social-justice matters, may be heard with new power in the Three-Year Lectionary, because Epistles now have a better chance than ever before to be heard in their own integrity, as they are read in a connected sequence of excerpts. The preacher has an opportunity to preach on an Epistle Sunday after Sunday, as seldom before. Since by and large the Epistles seem to have been ignored during the first round or two of use for the new lectionary, in favor of the Gospel for the Day or the Old Testament selection, there is now a chance to redress this imbalance by attention to Epistle selections.

Another limit to lectionaries as far as social justice is concerned is the obvious fact that the "right" passages on a topic do not always come up at the right time when current events demand they be heard. That is particularly true on specific topics. Regarding "God's Call to Public Responsibility," for example, the passages which might readily come to mind are Romans 13:1–7 and, one hopes, also Revelation 13, 1 Peter 2:13–17 and 4:12ff, and Acts 5:17–32. Yet these passages crop up in the Three-Year Lectionary for Pentecost A, never, never, Holy Innocents *and* 7 Easter A, and 3 Easter C, respectively.

If all these details seem hard to follow, the conclusion simply is that the lectionary is not systematically arranged to deal with justice issues. In fact, lectionary makers have probably been little concerned with "the church in the world and in society" in making their choices. The preacher who wants to deal with such issues may hope at best for *one* appointed lesson fitting a theme, to which may be added other appropriate Scriptures as part of the sermonic development. In other cases the preacher will have to choose the texts which fit the particular situation. (For pro and con on lectionaries, see *Interpretation* 31, 2 [April, 1972], especially pp. 139–53. To add justice as a concern is to introduce a topic with which few lectionaries have been concerned.) Yet to have a special "social-justice lectionary" would no doubt lead to imbalances in other directions. Sensitized interpreters, alert to needs, and a balanced diet of Scripture will always be what is needed. If the broad strands of all parts of the Bible are heard periodically, people will not be able to avoid Scripture's general thrust to motivate us toward justice.

THE LECTIONARY FOR JANUARY-MARCH, SERIES A

To turn specifically to the period between Epiphany and Easter we find that the bulk of Gospel Lessons in the A cycle come from Matthew, and that 1 Corinthians is the Epistle in Epiphany.

Considering that *righteousness* or *justice* is a key Matthean term and "Christ our righteousness" (1:30) can be said to inform a great deal of what Paul says to issues in Corinth, the content of the lectionary looks promising. But a new hazard in employing the lectionary for social-ethical interests emerges when we see the pattern of references to the word for "righteousness/justice" (*dikaiosynē*) in Matthew (RSV cited, with the term italicized):

3:15   "Thus it is fitting for us to fulfill all *righteousness*" (Epiphany 1);

5:6, 10 "Blessed are those who hunger and thirst after *righteousness* for they shall be satisfied . . . . Blessed are those who are persecuted for *righteousness*' sake, for theirs is the kingdom of heaven" (Epiphany 4);

5:20   "Unless your *righteousness* exceeds that of the scribes and the Pharisees, you will never enter the kingdom of heaven" (Epiphany 5);

6:1   "Beware of practicing your *piety* before men . . . " (Ash Wednesday);

6:33   "Seek first his kingdom and his *righteousness* . . ." (Epiphany 8);

21:32   "John came to you in the way of *righteousness*" (Pentecost 19).

All this looks very promising until we check a 1978 calendar, the year of this publication. Easter comes early, Epiphany is shortened to four Sundays plus the Transfiguration, and so only Matthew 3:15 and 5:6, 10 get read, together with 6:1 later and 21:32 much later in the year. The omission of key verses like 5:20 and 6:33 is not untypical of what happens all too frequently to the neat patterns of the Three-Year Lectionary: significant appointments are omitted because of calendrical considerations, often of a lesser festival taking precedence over a regular Sunday (to say nothing of "Youth Sunday" or "Scout Sunday").

A further problem, partly arising out of these calendrical considerations is that commentaries on the lectionary may omit treatment of those verses, important as they are for our purposes, which do not come up in a particular year. Thus Reginald H. Fuller's *Preaching the New Lectionary* (Collegeville, Minnesota: Liturgical Press, 1976) lacks treatment of Matthew 6:33, and Gerard Sloyan, *A Commentary on the New Lectionary* (New York: Paulist Press, 1975), where 5:20 is also omitted. Even where the lesson is treated, as in *Proclamation* (Philadelphia: Fortress Press, 1973–76) the exegesis may ignore the verse, as in the case of 6:33, though the homiletical interpretation builds on it.

What to do? When an interpreter comes upon a key theme in a pericope in the lectionary, he or she ought to trace it through the book or corpus of literature involved, even though the other pertinent passages are not in the lectionary or are not used that year. *It may be that a verse not read in the lectionary is precisely the one needed to make clear a passage that is read.*

A final comment before sizing up "justice" in Matthew: What does one look for in the Bible on social-ethical issues? There are skills involved in learning what topics, what situations, what analogies to explore which will be relevant to modern interests. A basic matter involves key terms and how to translate them and how to do a word study. All the methodology in an article in the Kittel *Theological Dictionary of the New Testament,* or its Old Testament counterpart, or briefer guides like Richardson's *Theological Word Book* can be involved, not to mention the intense debate on such issues.

For a starter, it is worth bearing in mind that a Greek or Hebrew term may be differently translated in different Bibles. Some renderings, particularly of Roman Catholic origin, because of the Latin influence, are likely to use the term *justice* at a point where Protestant ears are accustomed to "righteousness." This was true of Rheims-Douai in all these Matthean passages, and of Knox at 5:20, or of NAB in rendering Paul (cf. 1 Cor. 1:30, but "holiness" is preferred in Matthew). Conversely, where either term was familiar before, newer translations may have some free paraphase. TEV prefers "what God requires" (Matt. 3:15; 5:6, 10, 20; cf. 6:33), whereas *The Living Bible* speaks simply of "good" or "goodness" (5:6, 10, 20) or paraphrases considerably ("give him first place in your life and live as he wants you to," 6:33, which, to say the least, has individualized the text). The best advice is to latch on to a term which may be rendered "justice" sometimes, and work through other nuances and variant renderings elsewhere. *Justice* is a bigger term in Scripture than a concordance to a single translation usually shows.

"JUSTICE" IN MATTHEW

These preliminaries behind us, what can be said about this topic, on a word that occurs seven times in the first Gospel, every instance being almost certainly redactoral? (For details, see a recent commentary, such as that by Schweizer or Hill, listed below; or Kingsbury in Proclamation Commentaries, *Matthew*, pp. 86–90; or *Righteousness and Society*, pp. 67-71.) Obviously the theme Matthew inserts into a source (Mark, Q) or finds in his own special material (M) is an important one to him.

We must be careful not to read Matthew's uses of *dikaiosynē* in terms of Paul's meaning, around which much recent scholarly debate has swirled (cf. "Righteousness in the NT" in *IDBS*, which discusses only Paul). Conzelmann, in his *Theology of the New Testament* (1969), p. 149, has warned: "There is no correspondence between righteousness in Paul and righteousness in Matthew; the parallel is between righteousness in Paul and the kingdom of God in Matthew." Yet such a neat distinction seems to run afoul of the juxtaposition of "his kingdom and his righteousness" in 6:33. Is the former a gift from God and the latter an ethical demand (Conzelmann, p. 145)?

Another method of approach (Kingsbury) is to distinguish between "the righteousness of God" (6:33; 5:6) and the righteousness of the disciples (5:20; 6:1; 5:10). The former would denote God's "justice, which issues in salvation and judgment for humans," and the latter "doing the will of God," i.e., what is right, and bearing fruit. Yet 5:6 is at issue in several translations—is it fervent longing "for God to establish his just rule over all the world" (Kingsbury), to "see right prevail" (NEB), or "to do what is right" (NEB, note) and to possess "goodness" (Phillips) and "holiness" (NAB).

Still a third way of organizing the references is to begin with 21:32 and assume "the way of righteousness" as a salvation-history theme: Jesus and John the Baptist, and their Old Testament predecessors, the prophets, martyrs, and saints came as righteous persons, proclaiming and demanding righteousness. The church is that community upon which this imperative is especially laid, to seek justice and what is right. (Cf. the summary and critique of Strecker's view in *Righteousness and Society*.)

Commentators are agreed that 5:20 or 6:33 may be good starting points for understanding what Matthew means. Verse 5:20 insists that the justice shown by disciples must be greater than that of the finest advocates for the Judaism of that day, the scribes and Pharisees—greater in kind and not just in degree. This is to be done by disciples as salt and light in the world (5:13–16), in love towards the neighbor, seeking to be "perfect" (5:48; 19:21), i.e., whole or complete. That clearly indicates an ethical emphasis on doing justly.

Verse 6:33 is more difficult, for into the statement as recorded in Luke 12:31, "Seek his kingdom, and these things shall be yours as well," Matthew inserts "first...and his righteousness" as well as "all these things...." In each case the verb implies "Keep on seeking...," so the kingdom, which is future as well as present, is the object of an ongoing quest by disciples. "Righteousness" may be taken as a parallel to God's "kingdom," in which case both are eschatologically future and represent a gift God will one day bring. In that case, God's "righteousness" denotes salvation to come. The things to be "added" will be the kingdom and all it means. (Cf. the discussion in Schweizer, *Matthew*, pp. 53–56.)

In contrast, while such a sense for "righteousness" is well established in the Old Testament, especially Deutero-Isaiah, *righteousness* in Scripture can also mean "doing justice to another's needs, doing what God requires." Isaiah 56:1 combines this sense with the other when God says,

Observe what is right *(mishpat)*, do what is just (tsedaqah),

for my salvation *(qerobah)* is about to come, and my justice *(sedaqa)* about to be revealed (NAB).

In that light some commentators take 6:33 as more probably referring to "righteousness of life in agreement with the will of God" (D. Hill). Then Conzelmann would be correct: the kingdom is God's gift, in the indicative; the call to be just is God's ethical demand. Then "all these things," as in verse 32, refer to necessities for life which God promises to those of faith.

Whether in the term *righteousness/justice* of some Matthean passages, or in the emphasis upon the kingdom of God, one thus finds in Matthew first of all "gospel-talk" about God's good news *for us*, of what he *gives*. But then inevitably follows, in terms of "justice/righteousness" demands for *conduct*, ethical imperatives which are also part of Matthew's gospel message.

Careful study of these "righteousness-justice" passages will suggest that they call for disciples to follow in the way pioneered by Jesus and the Baptist. Further, that it is righteous action to be done in the world (6:1, but not ostentatiously; cf.5:16), and possibly that this action should be corporate and not just individual (use of "disciples" in the plural is probably significant). Here we have seeds for a social ethic in the Matthean community. The famous parable about how pagans ("the nations") who do not know the full gospel will be judged (25:31–46) suggests how wide the view of the Matthean church was, how world-encompassing its righteousness had to be, if it was to exceed that shown by the best of Judaism and the noblest of the Gentiles, to the hungry, the prisoners, or outcasts! The work for disciples is mapped out with devastating clarity.

We may ask, finally, whence these concerns arose within the Gospel of Matthew. One could, of course, point to the teachings of Jesus here cited, but these are selected and radicalized in Matthew as nowhere else in the Gospels. One could also point to the situation in which Matthew's church lived—coming into a new identity in the world sometime before A.D. 90—but that would only be a partial explanation.

A major factor must be attributed to the roots in the Old Testament and to the continuity with Israel's heritage which Matthew carries over in a way few New Testament authors do. A sense of justice and righteousness was inevitable, where the Hebrew Scriptures were revered and pondered.

The preacher today concerned about justice can find starting points in many of these Matthean verses about righteousness if the fuller picture beyond lectionary readings is kept in mind.

RIGHTEOUSNESS IN THE OLD TESTAMENT

The Greek word for "righteousness" *(dikaiosunē)* is usually used in the Septuagint to translate the Hebrew words *sedeq/*

sedaqa and to a lesser extent *mishpat*. How far these Hebrew words stand from our westernized concepts of righteousness and justice can be seen only in the contexts in which they appear in the Old Testament.

Most revealing of the difference between a legalistic, absolute understanding and the use of *sedeq/sedaqa* in the Old Testament is the story of Judah and Tamar which in Genesis 38 intrudes into the Joseph story. The woman Tamar had been married to Judah's first-born son Er. When this husband dies without having fathered children, Judah ordered the second son Onan to "perform the duty of a brother-in-law to her, and raise up offspring for your brother" (Genesis 38:8). But due to Onan's reluctance and subsequent lack of discretion, the Lord slew him too. Now it was left to the third son Shelah, who, however, was too young. While Tamar waited for Shelah to grow up, Judah forgot about his obligation, and so Tamar decided to take matters into her own hands. Dressed as a harlot, she seduced her father-in-law on the roadside, and she conceived. Three months later, as she was being taken out to be burned for becoming pregnant "by harlotry," Tamar indicated to Judah that he was the man. His response to her news in classic—and crucial to our understanding of *sedeq:* "She is more righteous than I, inasmuch as I did not give her to my son Shelah" (verse 26).

Righteousness therefore is a term of relationship; it is used for the satisfaction of obligations in a specific relationship in which the partners must be faithful. In the case of Judah and Tamar, the relationship is in the realm of family life and what is at stake is the law of levirate marriage. In another case, that of David and Saul, the relationship is political—perhaps even religious—and the issue is David's respect for the Lord's anointed king, which leads Saul himself to say, "You are more righteous than I; for you have repaid me good, whereas I have repaid you evil" (1 Samuel 24:17). People are involved in many relationships, each of which carries its own expectations of *sedeq/sedaqa*. Some of these relationships are, of course, personal; some are communal; some are national.

Over and above all such relationships in the Old Testament, of course, is the relationship God established with Israel—sometimes described by the analogy of the husband-wife relation-

ship (see Hosea) and at other times by the father-son analogy (see
Exodus 4:22–23). In this relationship righteousness is no different
from that discussed above: what God does faithfully for Israel
and what Israel does in faithful response constitute *sedeq*.

God's righteousness to Israel usually takes the form of his actions in the realm of history whereby he gives salvation to Israel
and establishes *shalom* for his people by giving them laws and instruction. Israel's righteousness to God is thus determined by laws
for orderly life that the Lord issues—not that they might by obe-
dience become his people but because they had already been
made his own. Even in this case, however, righteousness was not
a matter of an absolute ethical norm; on the contrary, depending
on the situation in which the people were found God issued new
commands for a life of *shalom*, sometimes superseding laws of an
earlier and different situation (cf. the updating of the Book of the
Covenant in Exodus 21–23 by the Code of Deuteronomy 12–26).
Thus the vitality of the relationship and the situation of the parties are determinative for righteousness.

RIGHTEOUSNESS AND JUSTICE IN SECOND ISAIAH

No theologian in Israel's history emphasized the centrality of
righteousness more than that prophet of the Babylonian exile we
call Second Isaiah. His preaching, recorded in chapters 40–55 of
the Book of Isaiah, makes clear that righteousness belongs first
and foremost to the Lord. This prophet stresses the dynamic
nature of *sedeq/sedaqa* above all in connection with the words
yesha'/yeshua' which are normally translated as "salvation" but
sometimes as "victory." In Isaiah 45:8 a little hymn calls on the
skies to "rain down righteousness" and to "let the earth open, that
salvation may sprout forth" which stands in synonymous
parallelism with "let it cause righteousness to spring up also."

Even more emphatic about the interrelatedness of salvation
and righteousness is Isaiah 51:4–8. In this section the parallelism
of *sedeq/sedaqa* and *yesha'/yeshua'* occurs three times: at verse 5
in reference to the immediacy of the Lord's act; at verses 6 and 8
in regard to the eternal nature of his salvation. In all three cases,
sedeq/sedaqa is translated in the RSV not as "righteousness" but

as "deliverance." The parallelism of righteousness and salvation is enhanced even more at Isaiah 46:13, where again the immediacy of the Lord's salvation is promised but now is added another parallelism: "I will put salvation in Zion, for Israel my glory." Thus the deliverance which the Lord is about to bring to exiled Israel will somehow result in the establishment of his glory in Zion.

This relationship of righteousness, salvation, and glory enable us to make several observations about the theology of Second Isaiah. First, in the context of Isaiah 40–55 these terms have something to do with the reign or kingship of God. Not only is the Lord portrayed at 40:11 as a shepherd of his people (a common royal image in the ancient Near East); not only is the Lord identified as the "King of Jacob" at 41:21; most important, the herald of good tidings who appears on the mountains "publishes salvation" and specifically "says to Zion, 'Your God reigns' " (52:8). The salvation of God (better translated here as "victory" as in Psalm 98) is directly related to his reign as king. And so, righteousness in the context of Second Isaiah has to do with the reign of God on which Israel can confidently place its hopes.

Second, the interrelatedness of our three terms demonstrates that righteousness belongs first and foremost to the Lord. In his address to Israel he speaks of *my* deliverance, *my* salvation, *my* glory (51:5, 7, 8; 46:13). So that there be no mistake about this, the prophet includes at 45:24–25: "Only in the Lord . . . are righteousness and strength; . . . In the Lord all the offspring of Israel shall triumph and glory. Thus only because there is righteousness in the Lord can the people of Israel experience righteousness. Only through him will Israel be established "in righteousness" (54:14). Indeed the righteousness of the Lord is nothing less than the inheritance which is given to the servants of the Lord (54:17).

God's righteousness thus takes the form of a gift to Israel. The gift is that deliverance/salvation of the Lord by which he accomplishes his victory and establishes his rule. At the same time, God's righteousness demands righteousness in return—as one would expect in a relationship of two parties. Israel is summoned to "pursue deliverance" (*sedeq;* 51:1); those "who know righteousness" are "the people in whose heart is my law" (51:7). Thus God's gift of righteousness goes beyond the act of salvation alone to include the gift of law *(torah)* , so that the delivered people under the rule of God can live a life of order in a right relationship with the Lord and with one another (see 42:21, Lent 3). Indeed, by keeping his commandments Israel could have possessed righteousness and *shalom* beyond comprehension (48:18).

In the first servant song and its expansion (42:1-7, Epiphany 1) it is "in righteousness" that God calls Israel and keeps her for the purpose of serving as a light to the nations, to open the eyes that are blind, to bring out the prisoners from the dungeon. Thus God calls Israel to righteous responsibility which goes beyond her own benefit. The specific task of the servant in the first part of this text is "to bring forth justice to the nations" and establish "justice in the earth" while "the coastlands wait for his law." Now righteousness and justice (Hebrew *mishpat)* come together. But what is *mishpat* in this passage? Some exegetes have interpreted the word here in a legalistic sense because of the parallelism with law *(torah)* in verse 4. Others have carried that concept further to mean Jewish "religion" in the sense that the mediator would instruct the nations in Jewish law.

While it is true that Second Isaiah himself uses *mishpat* in a juridical sense (see 41:1; 50:8; 54:17), the meaning of the term in 42:1-4 seems to be no different from the use of *sedeq/sedaqa* by this theologian. Just as the Lord was bringing *sedeq/sedaqa* to Israel in the form of salvation and *shalom* under his reign, so the servant (Israel in exile) was given the task of establishing the just order of life which will prevail for all peoples when God extends his rule universally. It is indeed appropriate that the addition to this song in verses 5-8 (unfortunately the lectionary for Epiphany 1 breaks off at the end of verse 7) ends on the note of God's glory which he reserves exclusively for himself. Thus here as in the case of *sedeq/sedaqa* at 46:13, the ultimate motive for God's action is the recognition of his glory.

The second servant song (49:1-6, Epiphany 2) picks up some of the themes from 42:1-7: the glorification of the Lord through Israel the servant, the reference to the call, the responsibility "as a light to the nations." There is added here something different: *mishpat* is not that which is to be established among the nations; it is rather that relationship with the Lord which the servant confesses confidently (verse 4), over against that lament in which the exiles without God cry "my *mishpat* is disregarded by my God" (40:27). Thus it is the relationship of *mishpat* that enables the servant to see beyond the apparent vanity of his situation to the future glory and universal salvation of God.

It is of no little interest that in the New Testament, particularly in the Book of Acts, the role of the servant in these first two songs of Second Isaiah is applied more to Paul than to Christ. Note the use of Isaiah 42:6 and 49:6 at Acts 13:47 (but see also 26:23) and Isaiah 42:7 at Acts 28:18—all in reference to the missionary work of Paul. The role of the servant in establishing justice among the nations and of bringing the afflicted into the presence of God is not therefore concluded with the historical Jesus but continued in the work of the church.

RIGHTEOUSNESS AND JUSTICE IN THIRD ISAIAH

The understanding of righteousness and justice in the preaching of Second Isaiah is continued and expanded by the theologian(s) we call Third Isaiah (chapters 56–66). In 61:10 (Christmas 2), *sedaqa* and *yesha* (salvation) again appear in synonymous parallelism as the garments which the Lord bestows upon the believer; in verse 11 *sedaqa* and praise are those responses which God will cause to spring forth before all the nations. In 59:16–17 righteousness and salvation are the garments which the Lord himself will wear when he goes out to gain victory over his adversaries. Thus in Third Isaiah these terms are likewise used to describe what the Lord does.

At the same time, however, this theologian of the post-exile period pays more attention to righteousness as Israel's response than to the Lord's actions—probably because the victory had already been won and the long-awaited deliverance had taken place. Therefore it is no accident that he begins his preaching in words not previously used by Second Isaiah: "Keep justice *(mishpat)* and do righteousness *(sedaqa)* (56:1). Because of the Lord's *sedaqa, mishpat* and *sedaqa* are now those things which Israel does.

But alas, the prophet finds that even in this new reign of God, established by his returning the exiles to Jerusalem, Israel only acts *"as if* they were a nation that did righteousness and did not forsake the ordinancy *(mishpat)* of their God" (58:2). The people complain that God pays no attention to their fasting, but God makes clear the kind of fasting he chooses: loose the bonds of wickedness, let the oppressed go free, share food with the hungry, bring the homeless into your home, clothe the naked. "Then shall your light break forth like the dawn, and your healing shall spring up speedily; your righteousness shall go before you, the glory of the Lord shall be you rear guard" (58:5–9a; Epiphany 5).

Israel's righteousness thus consists of caring for those who cannot care for themselves—not in order to be delivered but because God's deliverance *(sedaqa)* has already taken place. This doing of righteousness will fulfill that designated role of light to others (42:6; 49:6) and will thus give glory to the Lord.

All this is clear—*if* Israel would pursue righteousness. But the following chapter again makes clear that justice and righteousness are nowhere to be found (59:9, 14–15). All that can be seen are acts of injustice and unrighteousness: transgressing, denying the Lord, turning away from following God, speaking oppression and revolt, conceiving and uttering from the heart lying words (verse 13). It is when God sees there is no one to execute justice that he himself dons righteousness and salvation as weapons of war and goes forth to judge evil and to accomplish his purposes. On that eschatological day people from west to east shall fear his name and his glory (59:15b–19).

Thus, in the preaching of Second and Third Isaiah, it is clear that the Lord's righteousness takes the form of salvation for his people and the establishment of his reign. On the basis of his acts of righteousness God looks to Israel for a righteousness of her own which means freeing the oppressed, feeding the hungry, providing shelter for the homeless, entering the law courts honestly; these are some of the forms which righteousness takes for those who are delivered and who confess the kingship of God.

Even in this new relationship, however, God discovers that he has no righteous partner. There is neither righteousness nor justice to be found. But God's will is not dependent on the human partner, and so in spite of his people he sets out on his own to have his victory and extend his kingship over all humankind. No wonder then that when all this has been accomplished, the imperative goes forth to "seek ye first the kingdom of God and his righteousness."

FURTHER READINGS ON RIGHTEOUSNESS/JUSTICE,
ESPECIALLY IN MATTHEW:

Achtemeier, Elizabeth A., "Righteousness in the OT." Abraham Cronbach, "Righteousness in Jewish Literature." Paul Achtemeier, "Righteousness in the NT." *IDB-The Interpreter's Dictionary of the Bible* (New York: Abingdon, 1962), Vol. 1, pp. 80–99, especially 81–85 and 93.

Klein, Günther, "Righteousness in the NT." *IDBS-The Interpreter's Dictionary of the Bible, Supplementary Volume* (Nashville: Abingdon, 1976), pp. 750–52.

Von Rad, Gerhard, *Old Testament Theology* (New York: Harper & Row, 1962), Vol. 1, pp.370 ff.

Kingsbury, Jack Dean, *Matthew*. Proclamation Commentaries (Philadelphia: Fortress, 1977), especially pp. 86–90.

Hill, David, *The Gospel of Matthew*. New Century Bible (London: Oliphants, 1972), p. 96 *et passim*.

Schweizer, Eduard, *The Good News According to Matthew* (Atlanta: John Knox, 1975), especially pp. 53–56.

Reumann, John and Lazareth, William, *Righteousness and Society: Ecumenical Dialog in a Revolutionary Age* (Philadelphia: Fortress, 1967), especially pp. 67–71.

Abbey, Merrill R. and Edwards, O. C., *Epiphany, Series A*. Proclamation: Aids for Interpreting the Lessons of the Church Year (Philadelphia: Fortress, 1974), especially pp. 9, 26, 27, 29, 32, 34ff.

God's Call to Public Responsibility

William H. Lazareth

THE First Amendment to the United States Constitution protects both the free exercise and the nonestablishment of religion in American society. Professor Paul G. Kauper warns that a secularized culture tends to favor religion's nonestablishment at the expense of its free exercise, especially its free exercise amid controversies in the public sector of life.

Is religion strictly a "private affair" between the solitary believer and God? Does the free exercise of Christian faith and life play a significant role in the life of society at large? Is it unconstitutional for the church to express moral judgments on social issues that deal with the civil justice and common good of all the citizenry? Does the institutional separation of church and state mean the practical separation of religion and daily life? Must a pluralistic society silence the church's prophetic role?

Professor Kauper contends that the notion of religion as a "private affair" (Chief Justice Burger) must break down " as soon as the state protects the free exercise of the kind of prophetic Christianity which calls for public involvement as part of the church's divine mission." Our purpose is to substantiate that claim by appealing to Paul's Epistle to the Romans.

LIFE IN TWO AEONS

In one of the most profound passages of the New Testament, Paul encompasses all of human history by contrasting two opposing aeons represented by Adam and Christ (Romans 5:12–21). Adam heads the old aeon of death and sin; Christ heads the new aeon of life and righteousness. As he summarized it again to the Christians at Corinth: "For as by a man came death, by a man has come also the resurrection of the dead. For as in Adam all die, so also in Christ shall all be made alive" (1 Cor. 15:21–22).

Three theological convictions undergird Paul's position here. First, God's mighty act in Christ has cosmic significance. The cross and resurrection inaugurate a whole new aeon for humanity. Second, human life is linked inseparably with the lives of all fellow persons in corporate solidarity. Through birth all of God's sinful creatures are united "in Adam"; "through rebirth his righteous saints are united "in Christ." Third, sin and death are interrelated enemies of God. Persons die because persons sin; both are constitutive of the old aeon in Adam to be overcome by the new aeon in Christ.

Christians who do not accept the literal historicity of the first Adam can still appreciate the significance of designating Christ as the last Adam. Paul is lauding the personal and direct intervention of God in history to offer mankind a fresh start, a new beginning, a second chance. Adam depicts humanity as it is—in sin, law, trespass, judgment, and death. Christ represents humanity as it was meant to be—in righteousness, grace, freedom, love, and life. True human and true God, Christ came so that "grace might also reign through righteousness to eternal life" (5:21).

Later in this epistle, Paul also develops the paradoxical tension between the present and future dimensions of the Christian hope. On the cosmic level, the new aeon in Christ (the kingdom of God) is already inaugurated but not yet fully consummated. It has already intersected the old aeon in Adam but not yet replaced it. In like fashion, on the human level, Christians are at once righteous and sinful, already justified but not yet fully sanctified. They are simultaneously sinful creatures in the old aeon of Adam and redeemed saints in the new aeon of Christ.

Paul offers a realistic appraisal of the sufferings involved in the present aeon, as well as an affirmation of hope in the glorious fulfillment of God's will in the aeon to come (8:18—39). It is that hopeful realism which is the hallmark of mature Christians. Transcending the human alternatives of pessimism and optimism, Christians view both the depths of sin and the heights of grace in hopeful anticipation of the glory of God.

The sufferings of the present are characterized by a threefold "groaning." First there is the groaning of creation. Paul recalls that the ground was cursed by God because of the unrighteousness of Adam (Gen. 3:17). There is a witness here to the oneness of creation, the mysterious interaction between the realms of nature and history. The world of nature is also subject to decay and death. The apostle pictures it "in travail," anticipating its liberation in Christ and cosmic transformation into the long-awaited "new heavens and a new earth in which righteousness prevails" (2 Peter 3:13).

There is also the groaning of Christians. Paul develops the "already-not-yet" tension of Christian existence in which we have only the "first fruits of the Spirit" (8:23). We are already heirs with Christ, but in the present we have received only a down payment of the riches of God's bounty. The saints of God are not yet sinless and beyond suffering and death. Only by hope do we anticipate our full redemption.

Finally, there is the groaning of the Spirit. In a profound insight into the nature of prayer, Paul declares that God's Sprit intercedes for imperfect Christians who are both unable and unwilling to pray with Jesus, "Not my will, but Thine be done." Incapable of distinguishing clearly between our sinful wants and our righteous needs, Christians need the indwelling guidance of God's Spirit to learn how to pray according to God's will.

Yet Paul's final word is a cry of hope in the ultimate outcome of God's venture with humanity. The cross of Christ shows that "God is for us" (8:31). Nothing, therefore, can finally separate us from God's love in Christ. Indeed nothing short of cosmic reconciliation will satisfy the universal Lord of life.

SERVICE IN CHURCH AND STATE

After eleven chapters focused on the theological bases of the Christian faith, Paul devotes the remainder of his epistle to the ethical dimensions of the Christian life. He contrasts two forms of life for Christian guidance: be not "conformed" to the old aeon in Adam but rather be "transformed" to the new aeon in Christ (12:2). Christians have always found it difficult to distinguish these two aeons without falsely separating or identifying them.

Maintaining the tension between Christian discipleship and political citizenship has been especially difficult. Some Christians have betrayed the uniqueness of God's redemptive activity and the gospel by equating the new aeon with their so-called Christian nation, Christian constitution, Christian political party, and Christian legislation. Other Christians have denied the universality of God's creative activity and the law by severing the new aeon from a "Godless" state, "crooked" politicians, "dirty" politics, or "swindling" regulations.

Paul declares that Christian citizens, as both righteous and sinful, express their fidelity to God through both the church and the state. Hence, he incorporates the civic righteousness of responsible citizens ("you also pay taxes") within the Christian righteousness of reborn saints ("love one another"). In short, Paul's social ethic subsumes political justice under Christian love.

Paul's epistle shows that love provides us with the motive and direction but not the specific content of Christian social ethics. Faith first becomes active in personal love in meeting the needs of a single neighbor. Then love goes on to use reason and power to achieve more social justice for meeting the needs of many neighbors. Therefore, the biblically-exhorted "cup of cold water" may well take the modern form of a giant hydroelectric plant when a whole village lives in thirst on the edge of a desert.

Christians as citizens should welcome and support a just state in the realization that "there is no authority except from God" (13:1). This certainly does not mean the uncritical endorsement of any and every particular government or governor, especially an unjust dictatorship or ruthless tyrant. Christ alone is Lord! It is rather "governing authority" as such, which Paul declares to be the God-ordained means whereby the weak and innocent are protected "by the sword" against the oppression of evil persons.

Since not all sinners are incorporated in the new aeon in Christ, and since sin persists even in the lives of Christians, just governments remain one of God's most effective barriers against sin in the old aeon of Adam. However, if and when civil rulers no longer act as "God's servants" for political justice and degenerate into Satan's "beasts" in corporate sinfulness (Rev. 13), then with the courageous example of Peter and the apostles, "We must obey God rather than men" (Acts 5:29).

PUBLIC ADVOCACY FOR SOCIAL JUSTICE

The twentieth century has witnessed a glorious renewal of Christian concern for fuller manifestations of the church's total mission. Professor Kauper has rightly warned us of the dangers inherent in current slogans which state that "religion is a private matter," and "religion and politics don't mix." That divorce is likely true of many human religions, but it has nothing at all to do with biblical Christianity, as Paul has so faithfully demonstrated.

God is the living Lord of all of life. To exclude the crucial realm of politics from Christian thought and action is not merely ecclesiastical apathy; it is ultimately theological heresy and ethical disobedience. It is true that politics will never bring anyone to salvation. But it is also true that political life is the God-ordained pattern for preserving life in peace, justice, and freedom so that the saving gospel of Christ might be proclaimed to the ends of the earth.

Revelation, Liberation, and Revolution

This adapted material was presented as an addendum to the author's address (abbreviated above as "God's Call to Public Responsibility") in June 1977 at the Sixth Assembly of the Lutheran World Federation in Dar es Salaam, Tanzania. This was the first anniversary of the Soweto uprising.

The *Tanzania Daily News* recalls the tragedy for us: "One year ago, the racist police of John Vorster gunned down—on cold blood—innocent and defenseless children at Soweto. The unsuspecting youngsters were slain by the fascist armed men while peacefully demonstrating against the forced use of Afrikaans in school teaching. Today all progressive human beings are paying tribute to these children who died as martyrs in the cause of freedom and dignity."

Some foreigners at this Assembly have been stunned by the African response. "Uhuru war gets church backing," screams the headline in the same newspaper. Bishop Sebastian Kolowa is quoted as saying that although the church as an institution is not supposed to go into warfare, it fully supports the liberation struggle in Southern Africa because that struggle is defending the basic rights hitherto denied to the majority. Bishop Joshua Kibira said that once violence had been declared, the only choice open was to meet it with violence. "If I were confronted with a gun, I would not face the assailant with a Bible," he emphasized.

These characteristically "unchristian" statements being made by our hosts pose a challenge to the rest of us here as their guests. In 1977 we must be honest before God and the world. The proper interpretation and application of Romans 13 has plagued and divided Christians for the past four hundred years:

—from the official drownings of the Anabaptists in the 1530s down to the Nazi gas chambers for Jews in the 1930s;

—from the religious crusades against the "infidel Turks" in the 1520s down to wasting "Vietnamese 'gooks' " in the 1960s;

—and from the uprising of the peasants' rebellion in 1525 down to the guerilla warfare responses to the Soweto Massacre in 1977.

If, in the light of Romans 13, I am asked to recommend a clear word from Dar es Salaam to our suffering sisters and brothers everywhere—especially in Africa—I respectfully suggest a triple confession of corporate guilt: "We Christians have not witnessed clearly enough, either in word or in deed, about revelation, liberation, and revolution."

REVELATION

Christians confess in faith the revelation of the whole Word of God. Yet in daily life we have too often overemphasized the church's proclamation of God's gospel for heavenly salvation at the expense of its advocacy of God's law for earthly justice.

Reformation-based Christians have always been concerned about "the true treasure of the church—the most holy gospel of the glory and grace of God" *(sola gratia, solus Christus, sola fide, sola Scriptura)*. This has often led us to employ God's law only in its theological function (to condemn sins of unrighteousness), but not to champion also its civil function (to prevent crimes of injustice).

The twentieth century is not the sixteenth century, and to follow Reformation theology does not always mean the mechanical imitation of its time-conditioned accents. Luther's was an age of clericalism and his chief task was to put the church back under God's gracious gospel. Ours is an age of secularism and our timely calling is to put the state and society back under God's universal law. Without losing Luther's insistence that every Christian is baptized to become a priest in the church, we must also challenge every baptized Christian to become a prophet in society.

LIBERATION

Christians confess in faith the twofold rule of God as saving Redeemer and as preserving Creator. Yet in daily life we have too often overemphasized our freedom from "sin, death, and the devil" at the expense of our social and political liberation from injustice, oppression, and the violation of human rights and dignity.

The best Reformation research today documents the view that a correct understanding of the "two-kingdoms" doctrine involves obedient participation in God's activity in the world. Christians may credibly oppose a kingdom-building "liberation theology" only if they boldly advocate a justice-fostering liberation ethic.

This demands our corporate acknowledgment that advocacy for justice is an essential part of the whole mission of the church. All political systems are under sin and subject to divine judgment. The church can never truly be above the political struggle in a posture of neutrality. It must be prophetically active in word and deed within political power struggles. It dare not thereby lose its unique identity, but it must not retreat from its incarnational identification. Neutrality is a political myth: it is simply a covert way of uncritically identifying with the unjust *status quo*. At worst it is often little more than a convenient way to disguise the church's own political, economic, and institutional self-interest.

Advocacy for justice is inherent in the proclamation of the whole Word of God and is not merely a dispensable consequence of it. It witnesses to the universal sovereignty of God's law over all creation. He is the Lord of the nations as well as the Savior of the church. In discipleship to this Lord, the church is called to offer its critical solidarity with all persons created in God's image who witness to those remnants of God's law written on their hearts by their sacrificial struggles for human liberation, freedom, and justice in society.

I advocate critical solidarity: "critical" because all persons are tempted to act as sinners even in the search for more justice, but also "solidarity" because the human struggles for liberation—against racism, sexism, and economic/political oppression—are never limited to Christians alone and can never be won by Christians alone. We dare never be yoked with nonbelievers in the realm of redemption where divine liberation is a gift of God's righteousness. However, we must always be yoked with nonbelievers in the realm of creation where human liberation is a common struggle for civil justice.

REVOLUTION

Christians confess that faith-activated love must balance the conflicting claims of reason and force in order to achieve more justice, freedom, and peace in society. Yet in daily life we have too often overemphasized the right of citizens to engage in a "just war" as a last resort, in foreign affairs, at the expense of our participation, in a "just revolution" as a last resort in domestic affairs.

Christians are not romantic idealists; they are political realists. Paul taught that the sword has been delegated to Casear for justice. That is, in a fallen and evil world, force may be employed as a last resort when all reason has failed. I am emphasizing "as a last resort" because sinners are capable of massive self-delusion in defining the intolerable limits of oppression and injustice in an imperfect world. Nevertheless, it is justice and freedom, not order and stability, which are the chief goals of the civil community.

While Christians have rarely been ideological pacifists when it comes to engaging in what we consider to be a "just war," we have seldom championed the domestic equivalent of a "just revolution." Dictators have often thrived in our quietistic submission. We do not now even enjoy the prudential advantages of raising the threat of a "just revolution," whether or not we are actually able or willing to engage in one.

"Render to Caesar" must be obeyed today within the context of responsible citizenship in representative democracies. Rulers and subjects are no longer separate classes as in Paul's and Luther's day. In the present time when all citizens are called to act as "little Caesars," what prevents us from developing realistic criteria for revolutionary action "as a last resort" when all other attempts for peaceful liberation have failed? Christians in the twentieth century can no longer risk the ethical schizophrenia of endorsing armed struggle against dictators abroad but not at home. Parallel with the issue of liberation, we may credibly oppose a kingdom-building "theology of revolution" only if we boldly advocate a justice-fostering *ethic* of revolution.

Consider the situation in South Africa as one grievous case in point among others. Certainly Romans 13 teaches us to respect and obey legitimate civil authority as part of our responsible care of creation. In light of Revelation 13, however, is not the government of South Africa more and more losing its claim to both moral and legal authority? Does the institutionalized violence of the system of *apartheid* (racial separation) not "rend asunder" what God himself has "joined together" among black and white baptized members of the same community in Christ? Are we not approaching the time *(status confessionis)* when a united church fellowship must thunder its prophetic "No!" to the South African government in faithful witness to God's holy law?

For the final time, I am speaking of revolution, as of warfare, as an activity to be engaged in by Christians as citizens "in fear and trembling" solely when it is a last, last, last resort against the oppression of an illegitimate government. My prayerful hope, of course, is that as conscientious Christians and churches fulfill their advocacy for human justice and liberation more effectively, neither revolution nor warfare will be necessary.

Congregational Life

THE continuing task of a parish pastor is to set the members of the congregation on a collision course with the theology of the church. We experience this in questions which relate to the Second Article of the Creed, our salvation in Christ, and to the Third Article of the Creed, our life in the church. We also experience this in questions which relate to the First Article and the personal and familial dimensions of God's work of creation (better, creating).

To stop there, however, is to leave our people with a lopsided God and to withhold the perspective and encouragement which a full understanding of the word gives to their daily ministries and participation in society. When faith is limited to the "private" areas of life, it is faithless both to God's will and people's needs. This we know. The trick is in also knowing how to move into the areas described by Professor Kauper at the end of his essay: (1) religion as a "private affair"; (2) the public impact of Christians; and (3) the church's educational and prophetic role.

My experience and conviction are that we can do this effectively only if parish efforts are solidly grounded in evangelical theology, i.e. in the faithful development of the biblical and confessional heritage. The biblical and theological essays in this series are not merely perfunctory genuflections in the direction of Scripture as "response" to statements of current challenges from society as such. The parish pastor must always see himself or herself as the "resident theologian" for a group of saints who want to be equipped for their varied ministries. Thus, the affirmation of the

45

Christian's role as a citizen needs to be rooted in our understanding of the two uses of the Law, the different but not divorced functions of law and gospel, the left and right hands of the one God.

We must be clear about these distinctions in order for it to be possible for us to press hard on the "why" of justice while disclaiming secret and certain knowledge of "how" such justice can be achieved. The debate and mutual struggle for the "how" are better received and more effective when placed in the context of and distinguished from the "why". I am convinced that the pastor should seek to make regular connections between the two in preaching, teaching, and in the pastoral leadership given the congregation—the "bland leading the bland" is not the model of fidelity—but we must also seek to make those connections with integrity. The link of "therefore" between "why" and "how" must be as informed and clear as possible.

A decade or so ago a prominent New York preacher was characterized as being popular because his sermons never mentioned "religion or politics." No one would ever make the same crack about Luther. In the *Large Catechism,* for example, he stresses the place of government in at least three different settings.

In his explanation of the Fourth Commandment Luther declares that civil government is the extension of the parents' role, responsibility, and authority for providing the context in which children can live full and productive lives.

In his explanation of the First Article he lists the gifts of God the Creator: body, soul, life, reason, understanding, food, drink, clothing, spouse, child, house, sun, moon, stars, air, fire, water, birds, fish, beasts, grain—good government, peace, security!

In his explanation of the Lord's Prayer's fourth petition, Luther writes: "To put it briefly, this petition includes everything that belongs to our entire life in this world; only for its sake do we need daily bread. Now, our life requires not only food and clothing and other necessities for our body, but also peace and concord in our daily business and in associations of every description with the people among whom we live and move—in short, everything that pertains to the regulation of our domestic and our civil or political affairs. For where these two relations are interfered with and prevented from functioning properly, there the necessities of life are also interfered with, and life itself cannot be maintained for any length of time." And he even goes on to suggest that "it would therefore be fitting if the coat of arms of every upright prince were emblazoned with a loaf of bread instead of a lion . . ."

This kind of foundation both opens and prepares the way for a congregation to consider all kinds of political and societal issues. In the parish served by this author the Adult Forum has held series on bioethics (including contraception, abortion, genetic manipulation, organ donations and transplants, the "living will," and the prolongation of life/dying), on Namibia (including our government's African policies and the impact of multinational corporations), on the United States Bicentennial (civil religion, equality and pluralism, the nation-state and global interdependence, and the continuing revolution), and on the women's movement (including its implications for family life and business/career opportunities).

These series lasted from six to eight weeks at the same time as the Sunday church school. For all of them we established the theological context early in the series and kept it alive through all the sessions. We also arranged to have guest speakers who had special competence in the areas being considered. Every community has people who can and are willing to help a congregation study issues such as these.

In one case, our Forum program even led to an evening meeting at which the leadership of our local hospital discussed for the first time with the people of our community its recently-adopted policy about abortion. In another instance, it prompted our congregation to sponsor a Town Meeting with other local congregations and synagogues as the contribution of the religious institutions to our city's Bicentennial celebrations. At this meeting interested citizens and community leaders of all types discussed local problems and possibilities.

An Adult Forum series that relates particularly to the subject of this Justice Book has been held twice so far. In 1974 we met with the two chief candidates from our congressional district for the House of Representatives, and in 1976 we met with spokesmen for

the two major Presidential candidates. In both cases the series
began with a theological presentation affirming the God-given
mandate for the church to be concerned about the quality of life
society provides and the impact of our country in the world community. On the second week we formulated the list of questions
we wanted the candidates to address. On the third and fourth
weeks we met with them separately, discussing the same issues
with each so we could compare their answers.

The most significant result of programs like our Adult Forum is
the support they give to our evangelical insistance that all the
baptized have been called to be God's ministers in the world.
They raise our sights from concern about things like taking pen-
cils home from the office, to concern about the influence our people have on the policies and activities of their companies, unions,
and other organizations.

It has been said that the form of government we have is not a
natural law, like the shape of a rabbit's ears. Rather, it is the ac-
cumulated result of the decisions made by people over the years.
Things could have turned out differently in myriad ways. Life is
not like a roll for a player piano, with all the holes already punch-
ed out, so that we can only pump the pedals, but cannot change
the tune. Our people are punching those holes every day. This
series of Justice Books should help them punch the ones which
play the music of justice.   F.D.F.

The Church in North America

CHURCHES frequently choose to speak to major social issues
through ecumenical organizations such as the National Council of
the Churches of Christ in the USA. The NCC's Governing Board,
which consists of official representatives of the member
denominations, adopts policy statements and resolutions. The
former are more comprehensive, must be acted upon at two suc-
cessive meetings of the Governing Board, and carry more authority. Resolutions, which are directed at issues as they arise, must
be solidly based on policy statements. Nearly all policy statements
and resolutions reach the Government through a process of ad-

vocacy which involves special groups and divisional committees within the NCC structure.

Obviously, there are times when the Governing Board adopts official positions without the full concurrence of all the representatives of one church or another. The Governing Board at its May 1977 meeting adopted one policy statement and several resolutions which relate to social, economic, or political issues.

POLICY STATEMENT ON "THE UNITED NATIONS AND WORLD COMMUNITY"

Space permits only excerpts from the "Call to the Churches" portion of the policy statement. After expressing gratitude for the United Nations' thirty years of history the document calls upon the churches "to work for five essential objectives within the whole complex of United Nations organs and programs, and especially in relation to the role played therein by the United States Government:

1. *"The United States Government must give much greater weight to the principles and actions of the United Nations in shaping of United States foreign policy.* While every country's foreign policy is shaped largely by its own vital national interests, the United States should provide an example of a country which in the continuing process of redefining its national interests, considers the U.N.'s judgment on the issue at stake.

2. *The increasingly dangerous stalemate in United Nations work on disarmament should be broken.* While only member states can disarm, the United Nations can help induce states to stop the arms race which now reaches $300 billion annually. In order to begin to accomplish the goals of disarmament, the Nuclear Weapon States should make substantial cuts in their stockpiles of strategic weapons.

[Disarmament requires that nations substitute the goal of world order for that of national security. As a contribution to such a shift in U.S. foreign policy, the churches should educate their members about the costs, dangers, and illusions of the armaments race, with its tremendous expenditure of human and natural resources and its potentially catastrophic conclusions.]

3. *The rising demand for a 'new international economic order,' expressed everywhere in the less developed countries and heard by many people of conscience in the richer nations, must be met squarely and not buried in rhetoric.* The United nations is the only place where all parties to the required changes in worldwide capital transfer, productivity, income

distribution, trade, pricing and tax policies, and control of transnational corporations can express their concerns and contribute their ideas. The future allocation of food, energy, and raw materials and the protection of our planetary environment cannot be determined fairly and accepted widely unless the representatives of all the world's people share in the great decisions that must be made. Progress toward a more equitable distribution of the world's food supply must be accompanied by measures which make it possible for the peoples of the developing nations to increase substantially their own food production. The religious communities of the United States should press the federal government and private corporations to participate creatively in the development of more just and humane economic relationships.

4. *The United States government must take initiative in its own policies and in the United Nations to promote human rights throughout the world.* The United Nations has selectively condemned violations of human rights in some countries such as South Africa, Rhodesia, Chile, and the occupied Arab territories. But the United Nations has not been able to send missions to investigate or to criticize alleged or proven violations in such countries as Korea, the Phillipines, Indonesia, Iran, Syria, Uganda, Czechoslovakia, Argentina; Brazil, Uruguay, and the Soviet Union. While the United Nations has adopted the Universal Declaration of Human Rights and drafted a series of declarations and conventions in specific areas, and has organized the Committee on Human Rights, the machinery for enforcing these rights is still prevented from becoming effective. As church people we must work to see that the United States acts to correct this situation by ratifying the many accumulating U.N. conventions and covenants relating to human rights which are already in force. Further, our whole nation can provide an example to the world by ending our own neglect of and discrimination against the poor, ethnic minorities, and women.

5. *Efforts should be made to develop changes in the operation of the United Nations and its specialized agencies whereby the policies and programs adopted may be more fully implemented.* In this regard, both power realities and the pressures of the developing world must be taken into account in the policies and programs adopted. Religious bodies, utilizing their Non-Governmental Organization status, should seek opportunities to strengthen the role of the United Nations. Religious witness today should rest on the principles of mutual national respect and global interdependence, not on capitalist, socialist, or Third World hegemony. The objective should be to strengthen the United Nations system by revising and revitalizing its bureaucratic structures. In order to play their proper role in realizing these objectives, the churches must place a higher priority on working with their congregations on the issues discussed, on increasing the visibility of these objectives in publications, sermons, and community events, and most particularly, on providing ef-

fective liaison persons to maintain access to the United Nations as well as to demonstrate serious support of its work. In addition, church bodies should promote study of the United Nations' organizational structure and functions so that we may become more knowledgeable as we suggest ways to strengthen it."

RESOLUTION ON THE COMPLETE CESSATION OF ALL EXPLOSIVE NUCLEAR TESTING

The National Council, in this resolution, "commends President Carter for (his) new disarmament initiative, urges him to pursue a treaty for complete cessation of all explosive nuclear testing by all nations with unrelenting vigor and courage, and urges its program units and member churches to take immediate action to encourage mobilization of public opinion and encourage citizen action toward the accomplishment of these goals."

RESOLUTION ON PRESIDENT CARTER'S PROPOSED ENERGY PROGRAM

The Governing Board expresses its appreciation to President Carter and his Administration for the detailed and thoughtful Energy Program presented to Congress on April 20, 1977, and welcomes his decision to "defer indefinitely" commercial processing of plutonium and further development of the plutonium breeder reactor. The Board, however, registers uneasiness about the practical effects that portions of the energy program may have on the disadvantaged, and urges the Administration and the Congress "to take extraordinary care to ensure that those of our society who are already economically oppressed and politically powerless are not further victimized by policies tailored to benefit powerful and well-organized interest groups."

RESOLUTION ON HUMAN RIGHTS

Acknowledging President Carter's commitment to the application of human rights in United States foreign policy, and particularly with regard to countries receiving United States aid, and reaffirming its own commitment to human rights, the Governing

Board urges "President Carter to apply the same test of human rights equally to all countries in the world."

RESOLUTION IN SUPPORT OF STATES WHICH HAVE RATIFIED THE EQUAL RIGHTS AMENDMENT

In accordance with a 1963 policy statement on the Status of Women, the Governing Board "commends those states which have already ratified the Equal Rights Amendment, and all those working for ratification, and urges the other fifteen states to ratify the ERA as soon as possible" (as of the resolution's date ratification by three additional states was required in order for the Amendment to become law). The Board also required that national meetings related to the National Council be held only in those states which have ratified the Equal Rights Amendment, until the ERA is ratified or until March 1979, whichever is earlier. It also invited member denominations to do the same.

C.W.T.

The World Church

"Christ's presence can't be pinned down like an airline time table. All we can safely predict is that he takes us by surprise. Staying open to that possibility is what faith is all about."

"Christ's name is named not necessarily through an exchange of texts, but through debates over human dignity and the things that divide a nation."

"The gospel is a stumbling block for all cultures. The challenge lies in ensuring we stumble over the real obstacle, the claims of Jesus Christ and not obstacles we set up ourselves."

—Kosuke Koyama in *One World*, No. 28, pp. 7–8.

THE Sixth Assembly of the *Christian Conference* of Asia met in May 1977 under the theme "Jesus Christ in Asian Suffering and Hope." Here there was an attempt to discern Christ's presence within the agonies and the aspirations of the peoples of Asia. Asian Christians are both a numerical minority and a culturally marginal people. They are poor and powerless, and live for the most part among peoples who are even poorer and more powerless—hungry, homeless, unemployed, and illiterate. Yet the Assembly delegates affirmed signs of hope in people's movements all through Asia, the new theology growing out of these movements, the dedication of the young, and the bankruptcy of dictators. Christ and his saving grace become signs of hope for all creation and the entire human history.

Bishop Julio Xavier Labayen of the Roman Catholic Church in the Philippines stated: "This theology shows us how far we swerve from a faithful following of the Gospel if we separate religion and political action; if we propose a superficial apparent unity in the flock of Christ as an ideal and overlook the oppression of some members by others, if we do not opt for the poor and foresaken as Jesus did; if we confuse culture and Gospel, or the Kingdom and the Church; if we back out of difficult political choices because of inadequate ecclesiology; if we forget that faith without ideology is dead; if we forget, as Moltmann reminds, that Jesus died charged with being a blasphemer by the Jews and a rebel by the Romans, and that his followers must therefore clash with the religious distortion and oppressive governments of our own day; if we do not realize, finally, that our liberating work here is taken up into the coming of the Kingdom" (*One World*, No. 28, p. 3).

IN CHRIST A NEW COMMUNITY—SIXTH ASSEMBLY OF THE LUTHERAN WORLD FEDERATION, TANZANIA, JUNE 1977

If *community* is the key word in the Christian idiom of our day, then all Christians and groups of Christians are called to find ways to appropriate its full meaning for themselves. Is there a gulf between our words and our deeds? Is our concern for justice, peace, healing, and reconciliation in the world consonant with our day-by-day experience of "community" in our life together? These are questions we must constantly ask if we are to be effective and credible as Christians in the brokenness of the life we share with others in the world today.

"The church today must be like a tent, a moving church, as it goes in and out among the people to meet them where they are," stated the Reverend Zephania Gunda, president of the Central

Synod of the Evangelical Lutheran Church in Tanzania. The whole nation (Tanzania), he stated, is called to take part in "a war against the three enemies of the country: poverty, ignorance, disease." The church in Tanzania has "agreed to join hands with the government and as a united group of soldiers, is prepared to go to the villages and fight against the three common enemies."

Mr. Gunda said he saw this call to live in Ujamaa villages and share with the people of Tanzania in their ordinary lives, also as a call from God. "The church has absolute freedom to proclaim its message in the villages. Thus the big task of the churches is to teach in order to awaken the people's conscience to social issues." Further, he stated, "the eternal truth of God . . . must be sought, thus quickening the consciousness of the people so as to revolutionalize their thinking about developing their own lives and the nation in which they live." "Having been properly taught Christian responsibility for one's neighbor, Mr. Gunda was confident that his people would stop asking the question of Cain: "Am I any brother's keeper?"' (Lutheran World Federation Information).

The Sixth Assembly of the Lutheran World Federation called for universal suffrage in South Africa and urged its white member churches in southern Africa to recognize that the situation constitutes a *status confessionis*. This term implies that opposition to the present situation in South Africa is a matter which strikes at the heart of church teaching and that churches should as a matter of faith reject apartheid. The recommendation rejected the system of apartheid in these words:

"Under normal circumstances Christians may have different opinions in political questions. However, political and social systems might become perverted and oppressive so that to reject them and to work for change is consistent with the confession.

"We especially appeal to our white member churches in southern Africa to recognize that the situation in southern Africa constitutes a *status confessionis*. This means that on the basis of faith and in order to manifest the unity of the church, churches would publicly and unequivocally reject the existing apartheid system."

Also, the Assembly by unanimous vote issued a sharp protest to the "continuing threat to human dignity and the manifold violations of human rights by the white minority in South Africa, Namibia, and Zimbabwe." Addressing member churches of the

LWF, the statement called for their self-examination of human rights situations and asked that a report on their findings be sent to LWF headquarters in Geneva within one year (Lutheran World Federation Information).

WORLD COUNCIL OF CHURCHES AID TO LIBERATION MOVEMENTS

The World Council of Churches' decision in recent years to give aid to liberation movements strictly for nonmilitary purposes caused an outcry in the Western world. But in the developing nations it is seen that the church is at least beginning to practice what it preaches, by aligning itself with the oppressed.

The WCC's "Programme to Combat Racism" has also campaigned against Western investment in South Africa. Member churches of the World Council have been asked to join the WCC in withdrawing monies from banks making loans to South Africa and to put pressure on companies doing business in that country.

The Programme Unit on Justice and Service in the WCC's structure is made up of five commissions: Inter-Church Aid, Refugee and World Service; the Churches' Participation in Development; the Commission of the Churches on International Affairs; the Programme to Combat Racism; and the Christian Medical Commission. All five commissions are seeking to relate their work more effectively to the current WCC emphasis "Toward a Just, Participatory, and Sustainable Society."

The search for new means of sharing resources within the ecumenical fellowship, the breaking once and for all with the traditional concept of donor/receiver, the need for recognizing and protecting the fundamental rights of the growing number of refugees in all parts of the world, the struggle against violations of human rights, the work of material aid and responses to emergencies and disasters are some of the concerns of this Programme Unit.

A deep concern of WCC staff is that the principles adopted by the United Nations in 1974 with regard to the "new international economic order" have so far not led to new developments and that continued practical negotiations have been delayed. The

WCC believes member churches must be alerted to this issue, information distributed, and governments urged to work toward a new international economic order.

The main priorities for the Commission on the Churches' Participation in Development focus on three main goals: (1) to assist the churches to see life theologically in mission and solidarity with the poor and oppressed, (2) to provide support for the organization of poor and oppressed peoples, and (3) to assist the churches in their search for a "Just, Participatory, and Sustainable Society."   R.C.W.

Political Advocacy

IT is highly probable that each reader of these Justice Books is a pastor or lay leader, faithful to the church and its mission. That faithfulness is at least a dedication to reading and learning which involves commitment to the concerns printed on these pages. The biblical texts which have been reviewed are rich and fruitful, dealing with personal commitment. Baptism has given us a life in Christ that is to be yeasty, salty, and brightening. Preaching the Word and administering the Sacraments are marks of a congregation. There needs to be constant exhortation to the faithful to turn to Christ for forgiveness and renewal.

Yet the challenge to personal commitment is not always balanced by the full and corporate challenge to serve. Often those selecting preaching texts seem to have concentrated on the "holy life" of the Christian. There are not many verses about justice and our living out there in God's world. Professors Reumann and Mc-Curley indicate this in their survey of Matthew and accompanying Old and New Testament Lessons. It is not easy to unearth an emphasis on justice. They even suggest we may have to add other verses not printed in the lectionaries for a given Sunday in order fully to present the Word.

Life truly is relationships—personal, communal, and national. It is our contention that it is the "national" that is most neglected in the life of the church. We are not a nation like ancient Israel under the kingship of God, but we are citizens of a pluralistic and secular world with an elected Baptist Christian as President.

That's not a bad or evil situation, but it poses the issue of being an American citizen as well as of being a Baptist Christian. Sunday worshipers are people with national relationships. That has been quite regularly ignored in our congregations.

Have you ever noticed how many words have been written and spoken about church and state—words indicating the two are separated galaxies beyond hope of relating to one another? Yet in many ways there is a considerable similarity between the life of the Christian in First Baptist Church and the voter of Ward 3 in Iowa City. That same person needs both the word of forgiveness and the words of challenge.

Comparison will often show that apathy is common to people both as worshipers and as voters. They are as willing to let Washington handle governmental affairs as they are to let the pastor run the church—until the taxes increase and the Every Member Canvass appears. Really, why shouldn't we be urgently encouraging Christians to run for office, to join a political party, and to read the political pages of the local paper as well as *The New York Times?* Why shouldn't we be stating the secular challenge as clearly and as often as the call to repentance?

Professor Kauper's essay starts from the First Amendment, relating religious liberty and the establishing of religious bodies. It moves on to the tests of Supreme Court decisions and inter-pretations. He writes about taxes and the purpose of legislation. There is a clear reminder of entanglements that result when church and government interact. There is no way to claim com-plete and rigid separation. Yet because the church and your con-gregation are tax exempt does not mean that they are rendered silent as institutions. Kauper annihilates the theory that religion is a "private affair." Preaching needs to be very specific about this. We need to balance the challenge to be faithful to God with the exhortation to be an involved voter.

Yeasty, salty, enlightened people are needed in the congrega-tion and in communities. Church members can disagree even publicly on decisions about welfare, health insurance, energy, abortion, and aid to nonpublic schools. Agreement should not be expected here any more than on the best methods of evangelism. Similarly, the church can speak by the votes of congregational social ministry committees or by national churches in convention. These are not "Christian answers" but responsible expressions.

Justice hangs bleeding on a cross until the church works desperately for its shared reality. It is at that point that church members can find the action and the interaction so healthy in a full life. Affirming that balance will mean that the clergy must walk with the people. That walk can be risky. Being a Christian is risky. There is tension within the forgiven saint who continues to sin. There is tension within the registered voter who is silent. There are sins of omission in both kingdoms of creation and redemption. But look at the opportunities!

Look then at several specific examples of the corporate church at work through governmental (national) relationships:

—A denominational task force with a staff person works to advocate the sharing of our food with the world's hungry. Not to act corporately here would be to neglect to bear witness in an opportune way; justice would be silenced.

—Legislation may cloud the real mission of the church and its work in the world. For instance, a description of the church confined to teaching and preaching reduces the reality of mission. To accept the definition proposed by the Internal Revenue Service may well be avoiding an opportunity to challenge such an unbiblical limitation of the church's mission.

—Proposed legislation about criminal justice requires someone to speak for the church against theories of revenge and retribution. Here again, silence is neither pious nor golden. In this instance, lives may be isolated or limited because the church talks only about "holy things" on Sundays.

Or view such issues from the congregational viewpoint. Sermon illustrations damning political intrigue can be cheap shots, especially to a courageous leader in Congress serving the nation side by side with an agnostic. A visit to a senator in quiet conversation can bear much similarity to the hospital visit and to prayer with a member of the parish. Justice claims such balance, even as Jesus claimed it in the story of the Good Samaritan and in the story of the Final Judgment.

Somehow we need to work quietly and continuously to balance the demands of justice and the expressions of faith. Evangelism is living action *and* outreach to everyone. Strength is needed for the whole mission of the church. It is a matter of equal time *and* equal concern. These are days in church and society when we need to see our brother and sister in governmental service as workers for justice. These are days when the corporate church needs to be seen working for justice for every person.

We are part of a closely knit community and national life. Church members are related to and involved in community social justice. The corporate church is similarly related to national agencies working on issues of social justice. We are involved. The real urgency is to act and serve, not just react and criticize.

C.V.B.

LITERATURE

A THEORY OF JUSTICE
by John Rawls; The Belknap Press of Harvard University; 607 pages; $5.95

This book, first published in 1971, has been reprinted at least seven times, quite an achievement for a closely reasoned volume of 607 pages. It has been called "one of the most important books on social theory to have appeared in America in recent years."

It is indeed an important book because it attempts to avoid the kind of reasoning which has gotten the human race into most of its troubles in the twentieth century: the notion that justice is whatever is in the interest of my particular group—or whatever the courts claim. Nazis and Communists, student radicals, and members of the Ku Klux Klan have asserted that "justice" is what is in the interest of the German people, the proletariat, the people under thirty, and the white race. At least one distinguished justice of the United States Supreme Court has stated that the law is simply what the court decides.

Rawls claims that justice is essentially "fairness." We arrive at a notion of what is fair only if we try to forget that we are Americans or Germans, female or male, students or workers, white or black. We are "unfair" when we take into account our particular situation. We favor our children over other children, our sex, our town, our profession, our nation, indeed our religion.

In order to avoid this bias, Rawls proposes that we must imagine a situation in which people do not know to which particular group they belong. "No one knows his place in society, his class position, or social status; nor does he know his fortune in the distribution of natural assets and abilities, his intelligence and strength, and the like" (p. 137). This assumption Rawls calls a "veil of ignorance," and it is behind this veil that people can agree on the principles of a just social order.

Thus he is able to derive the following principles (p. 302):

I.   "Each person is to have an equal right to the most extensive total system of equal basic liberties compatible with a similar system of liberty for all."

II.   "Social and economic inequalities are to be arranged so that they are both:

    (a)   to the greatest benefit of the least advantaged, consistent with the just savings principle, [i.e. the long range interest of the human race, cf. pp. 284ff.] and

    (b)   attached to offices and positions open to all under conditions of fair equality of opportunity."

Assuming these principles, we can "see our place in society . . . *sub specie aeternitatis:* it is to regard the human situation not only from all social but also all temporal points of view. The perspective of eternity is not only a perspective from a certain place beyond the world, nor the point of view of a transcendent being; rather it is a certain form of thought and feeling that rational persons can adopt within the world . . . Purity of heart, if one could attain it, would be to see clearly and to act with grace and self-command from this point of view" (p. 587).

It is in the last sentence that Professor Rawls lets the cat out of the bag. "Your eyes will be opened and you will be like gods knowing both good and evil" (Gen. 3:5). The book could be called: "Be ye perfect even as your Father in heaven is perfect." But this exhortation does not give us a solution to our problems of justice. It merely restates the problem in the most stringent form. If we are to attain justice, we must overcome the selfishness and egocentricity which have characterized our life together.

Rawls bases his theory on the assumption that "a rational individual does not suffer from envy" (p. 143). He might as well base it on the assumption that the earth is flat. The history of the human race, indeed biological evolution, is not the story of discarding self-interest. "To act with grace" as Professor Rawls exhorts us is not the same as to act like a genteel university professor (few of us are all that genteel). It is to act rather with a power which does not come from assuming the veil of ignorance, but from the good news of God's totally surprising intention for the world as revealed in Jesus, the Christ.   G.W.F.

WHY CHURCHES SHOULD NOT PAY TAXES
by Dean M. Kelley; Harper & Row; 151 pages; $6.95

Dean Kelley makes a convincing case for nontaxation of church property and contributions to religious organizations. His arguments are nontheological and tied to the American constitutional settlement and fall under the rubrics of "pragmatic" and "prudential."

Kelley addresses this "tract for the times" to what he perceives to be a pernicious trend within government policy which would constrict the "space" for religious free exercise. One is reminded of Madison's warning: Governments by nature tend to define liberty as narrowly as possible. For Madison (and Kelley) the remedy is in the vigorous exercise of liberty within a pluralistic society. The American Bill of Rights guarantees such "space" both generally in terms of freedom of speech, assembly, and the right of petition, and specifically, in the right of religious free exercise.

Does the nontaxation of churches and contributions to them facilitate the proper functioning of church and government each within its own realm of competence? Kelley's answer is a resounding "Yes." Since government is not competent in matters of faith, it had best avoid entanglements with churches. Taxation is one such entanglement. Kelley suggests that, under the "free exercise clause" of the First Amendment, government may not possess legitimate power to tax religious bodies.

The author deals with two significant problem areas: the definition by government of "religion," and the influencing of public policy by churches. On the first, he notes the risk involved in adhering to a permissive and vague definition of "religion" but indicates that there is no alternative. Since government has no competence in religious affairs, it should not presume to define religion too narrowly.

As to the "chilling effect" of restrictions on public advocacy by IRS regulations, Kelley notes that the original legislative intent in restricting the activity of voluntary groups in this field was quite different from its administrative outcome (p. 71). He also notes the inequity inherent in corporations' being allowed to deduct the cost of lobbying from their taxable income.

This book is a significant contribution to the public discussion of church-state policy today.   R.J.N.

Beyond Naiveté and Cynicism

EVERY religious community in America, perhaps in the world, is today divided into at least two contending groups. For want of better terms, we shall call them *copers* and *changers*.

Copers are people who use their faith to deal with situations they consider impervious to any meaningful change. They are aware of the fact that the most important decisions determining their lives were made for them by others. Nobody asked them whether they wanted to be born. Their sex was not optional and neither was their race. In the language of the philosophers, these people are aware of the contingency of the most important facts of their lives. For this reason, they feel the need for some support system which will enable them to function in a world not of their choosing. As people get older, the experiences of life tend to increase their awareness of contingency and their appreciation for anything that will help them cope.

Changers, on the other hand, are people who use their faith as a basic resource to inspire, encourage, and empower them to attempt to improve situations which they see badly in need of reformation. Sensitive to the many ills and injustices of society, they are eager to bring about changes that will make the world a better place. Their religious community is for them a source of values and ever-renewed encouragement to keep on trying to better themselves and the world about them.

At present, these two groups have trouble talking to each other. This is as true among Christians as among other religions—as true in local congregations as in national and international councils of churches. The problem of the copers is a certain cynicism. Some of them have tried changes and discovered what Luther had discovered centuries earlier, "Changing is easy, improving is hard." Because of disappointments, they have lost the optimism they consider necessary to keep on trying. They are comfortable with the realistic, some would say pessimistic, view of the human race as reflected in the doctrine of original sin.

The problem of the changers is a certain naiveté about human nature and human efforts. They frequently believe that problems people encounter are the result of an evil system. They seem to hope that if men were replaced by women in positions of power, whites by blacks, old by young, WASPS by ethnics, rich by poor—the world would change dramatically and people would be loving and kind; injustice and exploitation would cease.

As we have indicated by the value-laden words *cynicism* and *naiveté,* we believe the Christian faith offers an alternative to these choices. *Justice Books* intend to discuss forms of that alternative. The faith should help copers to welcome change and changers to appreciate the necessity of learning to cope with situations which cannot be changed. We hope that this alliance of copers with changers, on behalf of love and justice, can be brought about by combining a realistic analysis of the problems which confront us with a faithful and confident application of the power and hope of the Christian proclamation. We want to look honestly at a controversial situation without a hidden agenda. Depending on experts in the respective field to provide a clear and competent analysis, we shall see what can be done in the light of the knowledge and power that Christ has promised.

In this way we hope that through *Justice Books* the copers will be helped because we will try to avoid naive and premature panaceas. We expect that the changers will be helped because we will advocate concrete measures for change and suggest ways in which Christians can become instruments of change. All in all, we are committed to the insight formulated in a prayer frequently attributed to Reinhold Niebuhr:

> "Oh God, give us the serenity to accept what cannot be changed, the courage to change what should be changed, and the wisdom to distinguish the one from the other."

G.W.F., W.H.L.